IMAGES OF ENGLAND

COALVILLE

William Stenson (1773-1861), the founder of Coalville, born in nearby Coleorton. He was a coal mine engineer and was engaged in a successful mining enterprise at Coleford in the Forest of Dean before returning to this area in about 1825, when he sank an exploratory shaft into the 'concealed coal' at Long Lane. Coal was reached in 1828 and the town of Coalville began to develop.

IMAGES OF ENGLAND

COALVILLE

DENIS BAKER, COLIN CLAMP
AND STEVE DUCKWORTH
FOR THE COALVILLE 150 GROUP

TEMPUS

First published 1998, reprinted 2006

Tempus Publishing Limited
The Mill, Brimscombe Port,
Stroud, Gloucestershire, GL5 2QG

British Library Cataloguing in Publication Data.
A catalogue record for this book is available from the British Library.

ISBN 0 7524 1599 X

Typesetting and origination by Tempus Publishing Limited
Printed in Great Britain

Contents

Acknowledgements

The Coalville 150 Group wish to thank all who have made material available for inclusion in this book. While every effort has been made to acknowledge copyright of photographs included we apologize for any omissions made through ignorance. We would especially like to mention assistance given to us by Leicestershire Museums Service, Mr P. Smith, Mr C. Matchett, Mr R. Black, Mr W. PlattsMr P. Jacques, Mr E. Jarvis, Motors (Coalville) Ltd, Mr E.K. Deeming, Mr R. Butler and Mrs S. Hammond (for permission to include some of her late father Mr G. Lumb's photographs).

The Coalville 150 Group was formed in 1983 to celebrate the 150th anniversary of the founding of Coalville. It staged a large exhibition of artifacts and photographs at the local technical college and, following the exhibition, the group decided to continue with the aim of collecting, maintaining and developing a permanent photographic archive. In addition it sought to liaise with other groups in the town, foster a sense of community in Coalville and put Coalville on the map historically. Its long-term wish is to see a Coalville Museum established. Over the years since its inception the group has amassed a large archive of photographs of the area, selections of which have appeared in the Community Gallery at Snibston Discovery Park. The group has also published a town trail and several books about Coalville. It has designed and helped to produce a popular series of historical calendars and provides a regular newsletter, *Coalville 150 Group Digest*, for its members.

Introduction

On Saturday 27 April 1833, the locomotive 'Samson', driven by Robert Stephenson, arrived at the Railway Hotel on Long Lane pulling a train of coal wagons. This signalled the beginning of the growth of a new industrial town called Coalville. Coalville was built on an area of wasteland which comprised the distant corners of adjoining parishes of Whitwick, Hugglescote, Snibston and Swannington. These parishes were separated approximately north/south by Long Lane and east/west by Mantles Lane and Hugglescote Lane.

The development of Coalville can be justly credited to William Stenson who, at Long Lane, sank the first coal shaft into the previously unexplored and concealed coal measures by breaking through a subterraneous layer of Charnwood stone which overlaid the coal. Having established access to this considerable new resource of marketable coal, he then had to find means to transport it to Leicester. Having visited the Stockton to Darlington Railway and conferred with locomotive manufacturers, he returned to survey a possible route before seeking the support of John Ellis of Leicester. Stenson commented to John Ellis, 'Our carting beats us but I can see my relief if we can but get up a railway company'. This influenced John Ellis to visit George Stephenson at Liverpool and, on his return to Leicester, he called a meeting on 12 February 1829 which agreed to consider the initiative. An Act of Parliament was obtained in 1830 and this enabled the setting up of the Leicester and Swannington Railway Company to which Robert Stephenson was appointed as engineer.

During construction of the railway the Snibston Estate was offered for sale and Robert persuaded his father and two Liverpool associates to buy it in 1831. George Stephenson moved into the district to supervize the sinking of the first Snibston shaft, close to Stenson's Colliery, using a new technique involving cast-iron shaft lining to overcome the considerable water problems. He broke through the Charnwood stone, which Stenson had previously encountered, and subsequently sank a second shaft some distance to the west to avoid it. He was thus ready, with Stenson, to take advantage of the arrival of the railway in 1833.

Unlike Stenson, whose mine had been developed in the parish of Whitwick and who was able to employ local miners from a declining, exposed coal field just to the north, Stephenson had to attract miners from further afield. According to Samuel Smiles he constructed, adjacent to his mine in Snibston parish, 'a village of comfortable cottages each provided with a snug little garden' and for his workforce, 'a school which was also used by the Methodists for Sunday worship'. A contemporary resident of the new settlement, Samuel Fisher, later reminisced that the principal building in the area was the Olde Red House, which gave its name to the area, and which stood at the crossing of the roads named above before the town began. He remembered the construction of Stephenson's Rows and the development of that early settlement in 1832. Meanwhile, William Stenson needed to attract more workers many of whom were accommodated in Coalville Place (Club Row) and Stone Row, built close to Whitwick Colliery by the newly formed Coalville Building Club. Not wishing to be outdone by Stephenson, Stenson, who was a staunch Baptist, gave land and personal support for the building of 'a neat chapel in which a school was constructed on the Lancastrian system. It was attended by 120 scholars, principally colliers' children, the expense of whose education is paid for by Whitwick Colliery Co.'

The community continued to grow piecemeal along the existing roads and adjacent to new industries which supported or were supported by the mines and railway. Housing was erected to provide for workers in an iron foundry, several brick and tile works, and a wagon works, which by the turn of the century employed 1,000 men and boys. A large locomotive depot was also set up when the Midland Railway took over the Leicester and Swannington Railway Co. in 1846.

At nearby Bardon, Messrs Ellis and Everard developed a large stone quarry in 1857 and built an adjacent industrial hamlet. Coalville became connected with further railways in 1874 by the extension of the Ashby to Nuneaton Joint Railway and in 1883 by the building of the Charnwood Forest Railway. This connected the area with Loughborough and new traders came as the town grew, thus augmenting the services provided from the four parishes and ensuring that Coalville rapidly became an important centre of trade.

The churches established in the four parishes were all at some distance from the centre of the new settlement of Coalville, so a new church and school were built in 1838, although they were not dedicated until 1840 for want of an endowment. Other churches and chapels followed and these religious communities became the centres of cultural as well as spiritual enrichment for the townsfolk, providing facilities for four large mixed choirs, two male voice choirs, three full orchestras and several brass bands. The chapels also had their own football and cricket teams. Coalville Athletics Club organized and promoted regional sports meetings and cycle races and eventually donated land for the provision of a town park.

As local businessmen made their fortunes, they reinvested in the town through both land and leisure development, ensuring the availability of sufficient housing for the families of female workers in the industries that developed later, such as manufacturing boots and shoes, elastic web, elastic web machinery and clothing. For the peoples' entertainment, theatres, an electric theatre and a skating rink were provided.

The town was devastated in 1898 by a disaster at Whitwick Colliery when thirty-five men lost their lives in an underground fire. However, the community recovered sufficiently to welcome in the new century with a new found optimism under its own local government and illuminated by its own gas supplies. Coalville gained its own water supplies in 1904, which helped to eliminate epidemics which had wiped out whole families living in the crowded rows. In 1900, sixty-seven years since its beginning, the community had grown to 15,000 souls who faced the future full of optimism but were unprepared for the further difficulties they would face in the shape of the First World War and the subsequent recession, leading to the general strike of 1926. A newly formed Working Men's Co-operative Society flourished rapidly and supported the community through those difficult times. When the town commemorated its fallen heroes by building the Memorial Clock Tower, in 1925, alongside the Olde Red House it was belatedly signalling its importance in economy of the county of Leicester.

One

Earlier Times

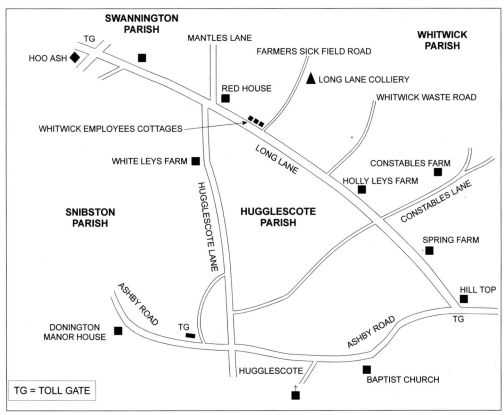

SWANNINGTON PARISH

TG

HOO ASH ◆

MANTLES LANE

WHITWICK PARISH

FARMERS SICK FIELD ROAD

■

▲ LONG LANE COLLIERY

RED HOUSE
■

WHITWICK WASTE ROAD

WHITWICK EMPLOYEES COTTAGES ■■■

LONG LANE

SNIBSTON PARISH

WHITE LEYS FARM ■

CONSTABLES FARM ■

HOLLY LEYS FARM ■

HUGGLESCOTE LANE

HUGGLESCOTE PARISH

CONSTABLES LANE

SPRING FARM ■

HILL TOP ■

TG

ASHBY ROAD

DONINGTON MANOR HOUSE ■

TG ■

ASHBY ROAD

HUGGLESCOTE

✝ ■

BAPTIST CHURCH ■

TG = TOLL GATE

A map of the four parishes.

Main Street, Hugglescote, c. 1870. Hugglescote was an ancient farming village which had its own watermill. This early photograph shows the old Manor House on the left and in the distance is an early farm, now demolished, which was owned by the Dennis family who were prominent Baptists.

The Market Place, Whitwick, c. 1890. Whitwick's origins go back to the Saxon period and a castle was built there in Norman times. Its Market Charter dates from 1288.

The Railway Inn, Swannington, *c.* 1900. The Leicester and Swannington Railway Co. carried out business here from 1833. Mining, which had continued in the village for 700 years, ceased in the 1870s with the development of the coalfield based on Coalville.

The Manor House, Donington le Heath, *c.* 1960. The Manor House was built in the late thirteenth century, probably on the site of an earlier building, and was in the ownership of the Villiers and then the Hastings families. Further alterations were made to the building in the seventeenth century and the house, which was described in 1964 as the oldest inhabited building in the country, is now preserved as a museum by the county council.

St Mary's chapel, Snibston. This very early chapelry, in a scattered village, was at one time given by Earl Leofric to the Abbey of Coventry.

The Independent chapel, Bardon, is the oldest Free Church in Leicestershire. Built about 300 years ago, it provided an opportunity for non-conformist worship outside the control of the established Church following the Toleration Act. The original chapel was altered in 1877, and is now cared for by a preservation trust.

The Olde Red House, *c.* 1900. The house was established in the area before the mid-eighteenth century and for many years its name denoted to people in other counties, the place of residence of folk from this area. It was also locally known as the 'Cradle and Coffin'.

White Leys Farm, *c.* 1890. This farm, in Snibston parish, was owned in the eighteenth century by the Orton family who farmed much of the district and also had a tannery at Swannington. Local entrepreneur James Gutteridge developed much of its land in the early part of this century.

The Birch Tree Inn, Bardon, *c.* 1950. This inn was built at Hill Top where Long Lane branched from the Leicester to the Ashby Turnpike through the area which later became Coalville. A turnpike gate and side bar were installed here in the 1760s.

Hoo Ash Farm, *c.* 1900. This was built at the western end of Long Lane where it was crossed the Hinckley to Melbourne Turnpike. A turnpike gate stood near the farm which was improved by Henry Burton in 1853.

Two

Beginnings of Coalville

A woodcut print from Samuel Smiles' *Life of George Stephenson* gives the earliest impression of the developing town of Coalville as seen from the track leading to Swannington Incline in 1845. Some of town's earliest houses, on Club Row, can be seen on the left with Snibston's No. 1 pit adjacent. The new church and houses, built for the wagon works, and Snibston Colliery school can be seen on the right.

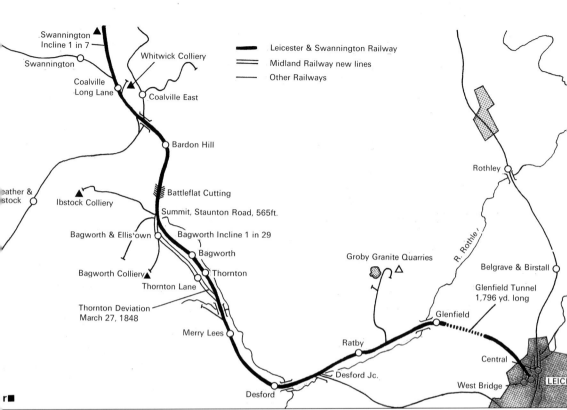

A map of the Leicester and Swannington Railway. The line, surveyed and promoted by William Stenson, was built under the supervision of Robert Stephenson by The Leicester and Swannington Railway Company. It reached Long Lane in 1833 and was the first railway to be built in the Midlands.

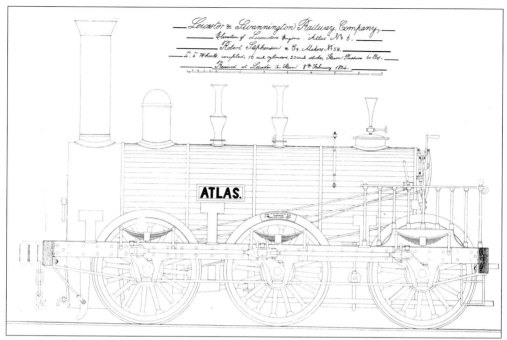

Leicester and Swannington Railway engine *Atlas*. This, the sixth engine to work on the line, was delivered in February 1834 from the works of Robert Stephenson. It had 16 inch diameter cylinders with a stroke of 20 inch and at 17 tons in weight it was, at that time, the heaviest engine running on any railway. It was found to be very suitable for duty at Coalville. After working for twenty-five years on this line, the engine was hired out to local collieries for a further fifteen years before being scrapped.

Snibston Colliery, No. 2 pit, *c*. 1910. While supervizing the construction of the Leicester and Swannington Railway, Robert Stephenson alerted his father to the fact that the Snibston Estate was for sale. George Stephenson organized its purchase and initiated the setting up of the Snibston Colliery Co. The company's No. 1 pit was sunk near to Stenson's Colliery in 1832 and the No. 2 pit was sunk on the Snibston part of Long Lane in 1833. Six rows of houses were constructed adjacent to this mine, to house incoming workers.

Whitwick Colliery, No. 6 pit's engine house and offices, *c.* 1930. The colliery was set up by a partnership of William Stenson, James Whetstone and Samuel Smith-Harris in 1827, but by 1860 it was in sole ownership of Joseph Whetstone, James' nephew. Both he and his son further developed the site.

Club Row, later known as Coalville Place, *c.* 1950. These houses were erected by Coalville Building Club on land purchased by William Stenson in 1839. The site was opposite the colliery and proved a good location to accommodate Whitwick Colliery workers.

Ashby Road, c. 1950. The rows of houses on the left were built by Snibston Colliery and were called Snibston Buildings No. 1 (known as George's Row), and Snibston Buildings No. 2 (known as Hetton's Row). No. 1 (also known as Deputies Row), was built for six of the colliery's supervisory staff and No. 2 (also known as Barrack Row), was built in the form of twenty-four back-to-back houses.

Snibston Buildings No. 3 (known as Upper Buildings or Long Row), c. 1960. This row comprised twenty-five two-up, two-down cottages built adjacent to James Place, named after George Stephenson's brother who was the colliery's first manager.

The rear of Snibston Buildings No. 6 (known as Snibston Buildings West), c. 1960. These houses also provided welcome accommodation for eighteen more families coming to work at the colliery from outside the district. The row, together with neighbouring Lower Buildings, was later renamed Kimberley Row.

Ebenezer Baptist chapel, *c.* 1914. This building housed the Snibston Colliery school which was erected by the company, 'for the education of colliers and their families'. It was used for Sunday worship and Sunday school by the local Methodists until 1865 and was purchased by the Ebenezer Baptists in 1879. Later development enlarged it further in 1881 and 1905.

Snibstone New Inn, dressed for King George V's coronation in 1911. It was built at the same time as the Snibston Rows, and it is said that the original intention was to call the new settlement 'New Snibston', but the signwriter mixed up the inn's name and spelt it incorrectly.

Ashby Road Station Hotel, viewed from the Midland Railway Bardon Hill station, *c.* 1930. The hotel was erected in 1832 at the point where the Leicester and Swannington Railway crossed the Leicester to Ashby turnpike road. Both overnight accommodation and staging facilities were available to travellers going to Ashby and other important destinations in the district. The fares to Leicester by train were 9d (closed carriage) and 6d (open).

The Railway Hotel, Station Street, *c.* 1880. This building, one of the first in the new settlement, provided travellers on the new railway with booking office facilities, accommodation and an opportunity to hire a horse for further passage.

Leicester and Swannington Railway tickets were made of brass and were given in token of the transaction for a journey booked. They were collected by the train guard at the destination and returned to the point of departure as proof of the completed transaction.

Swannington Incline engine house, c. 1930. The engine house was erected in 1833 at the summit of a 1 in 17 incline leading down to the village's collieries. The building housed an engine which is now preserved in the Railway Museum at York. Today, the site is preserved by Swannington Heritage Trust.

Swannington Incline winding engine, c. 1880. This single cylinder, horizontal engine was constructed by the Horseley Coal and Iron Co. at a cost of £750 in 1833. It powered a rope drum to haul wagons of coal up the incline for passage on to Leicester.

Swannington Incline, which had a single standard gauge track, extends for about three-quarters of a mile to the lower level. Coal was brought to the foot of the incline by horse-drawn tramways which came from the mines in the village and from others to the north. The track was little used by the late 1860s, with the closure of the village's mines, but was brought into more regular use again in 1877, because of the need to let coal down from Coalville to fuel a large pumping engine installed in one of the disused mines. This operation continued until 1947.

Coalville Baptist church and school, *c.* 1906. This was built in 1835 on land given by the Whitwick Colliery Co. Initially under the control of the Hugglescote Baptist church, the members separated in 1856 and the building was considerably enlarged in 1861 with the addition of a larger British School.

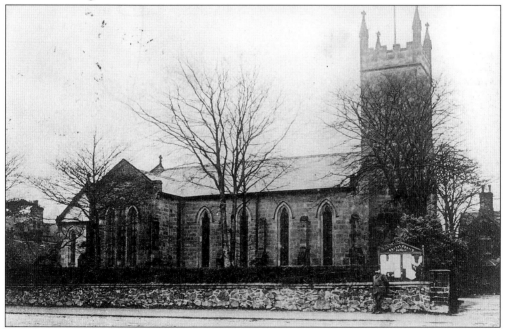

Coalville Christ Church and vicarage, *c.* 1915. The church and adjacent National School buildings were erected in Hugglescote parish on land provided by William Stenson between 1837 and 1838 at a cost of £1,400. However, the church was not dedicated for use until 1840 for want of an endowment.

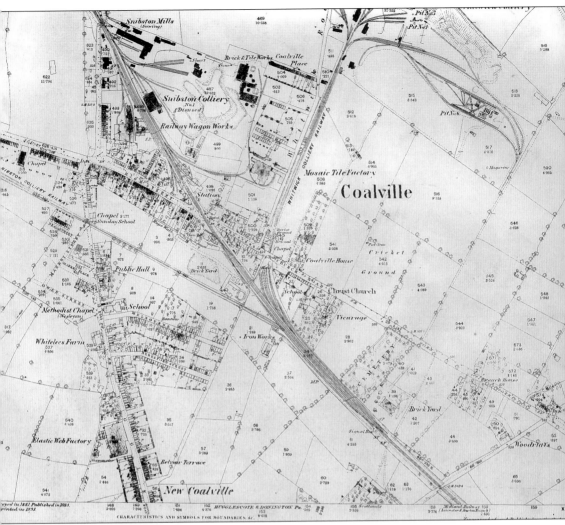

A map showing the layout of Coalville in 1881.

Three

Industry and Employment

'Snap time' underground, *c.* 1950. Miners at Snibston Colliery enjoying a well earned refreshment break.

Miners working underground in one of the local mines, *c.* 1920.

Two deputies going on their inspection round of the underground workings, *c.* 1920.

'Sailor', the winner of 3rd prize at Ashby Show, in 1933. Pit ponies were used underground to haul trucks of coal from the coal face to the underground rope haulage system which then transferred coal to the pit bottom. The ponies often lived and were stabled underground for the whole of their working lives.

Snibston Colliery pit top, c. 1940. Loaded tubs, which have been wound up the pit-shaft, are being removed from the two-deck cage.

Whitwick Colliery, c. 1920. A railway siding from the colliery led on to the Charnwood Forest Railway.

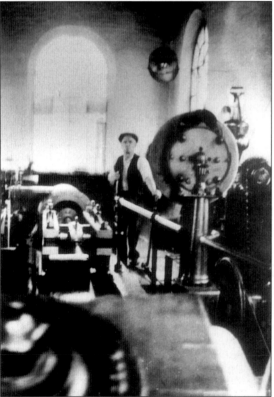

Bill Jarvis at Whitwick Colliery's No. 3 pit winding engine in 1933. 'New Pit', as it was known, was sunk in 1901. Mine engine drivers were highly skilled and competent workers on whom both the mine's profitability and the lives of hundreds of workers depended every day. Traditionally, their engines and engine houses were maintained in spotless condition. They could be said to have been the equivalent of today's airline pilots.

Harry Underwood, a coal 'higgler', taking the first load of coal from Snibston Colliery weigh-bridge after the 1926 miners' strike. The higglers collected coal from the land sales office to sell to local customers. For many centuries, higglers used packhorses to carry coal from other collieries to markets situated many miles away.

Miners waiting for their bus, c. 1914.

Whitwick Colliery rescue team in 1913. Rescue teams, formed from groups of the district's experienced miners, were highly trained to deal with situations where men were trapped underground. Each colliery had its own rescue team like the Whitwick team shown here with its instructor Mr B. Wilson at the Ashby Mines rescue station.

Whitwick Colliery ambulance team in 1938. Teams were trained at each colliery to provide expert first aid for miners involved in underground accidents. Whitwick Colliery team won many trophies in first aid competitions; on this occasion they won the Leicestershire and South Derbyshire Collieries Ambulance Challenge Shield.

Coalville's first railway station, c. 1870. The Midland Railway Co. took over the Leicester and Swannington Railway in 1846 exchanging a £100 share in the Midland Railway Co. for each £50 share of the Leicester and Swannington Railway Co. The new company built this first station at the point where the railway crossed the old Long Lane.

The Midland Railway signal box, level crossing gates and footbridge, c. 1906. A footbridge was erected in 1851 to minimize delays to pedestrian traffic caused by the numerous daily closures of the gates and, in 1856, the Midland Railway Co. introduced wire operated signalling, controlled from the signal box.

The signal box, *c.* 1915. In 1907, the box was elevated by the Midland Railway Co. to provide a better line of sight above the footbridge.

Coalville railway station, *c.* 1920. The station was much improved by the Midland Railway Co. in 1898 to cope with the considerable increase in trade.

First aid staff at the Midland Railway station, *c.* 1916.

Railway Terrace, *c.* 1960. The Midland Railway Co. provided this row of cottages in 1846 to house some of the considerable number of workers arriving to operate the company's depot in town. The larger house gave status to the supervisor.

A Midland Railway 0-6-0 Johnson engine at Coalville railway station, *c.* 1900. These engines worked out of Coalville for over ninety years until the last days of steam. The engine was particularly suitable for traversing the narrow Glenfield tunnel.

Coalville locomotive sheds and coaling stage, *c.* 1960. Coalville Locomotive Depot provided servicing facilities for up to nine engines and employed several hundred men and boys.

Coalville East railway station, *c.* 1960. This station served passengers on the Charnwood Forest Railway, which was incorporated in 1874 but not opened until 1883. The line connected the junction of the Ashby and Nuneaton Joint Railway and the Midland Railway, via a single track to the town of Loughborough.

The siding from Whitwick Granite Co. at its junction with the Charnwood Forest Railway in 1962. The quarry line provided a much needed service for freight traffic. The bridge in the distance shows that there was an initial intention to lay double track but the railway was never a sufficient commercial success to warrant this.

A special enthusiast's train, *c.* 1962. The Coalville East railway station foreman stands ready to exchange the single line token with the driver of one of the last trains to run on this line. The railway was absorbed by the LMS Railway Co. in 1923, closed to passengers in 1931 and was finally closed down and dismantled in 1963.

Stableford's engineering works, *c.* 1965. The old workshops of Snibston No. 1 pit, located on Mantle Lane, and the associated brickworks were taken over by J.W. Stableford in 1865. The engineering works, with sidings onto the railway, were taken over by W.D. Stableford in 1879 and further expanded in 1884 to concentrate on the manufacture of railway rolling stock.

J.W. Stableford and his family at their home on London Road next to Christ Church around 1890. J.W. Stableford concentrated on the sawmilling and brickmaking part of the business.

Stableford's forge shop, *c.* 1910. Many workers came to the town from the West Midlands to produce castings in brass and iron and to make specialist metal forged items. The workforce had expanded to over 1,000 by the turn of the century.

Workers in Stableford's press shop, *c*. 1910. They produced items for wagon construction and chains for railway, mining and naval customers from Africa, India and the Far East. Stableford's also recruited staff for the Indian Railways.

A Stableford oil tanker wagon, *c*. 1920. These specialized products were exported for use in the newly developing Middle East oil fields. Evidence of their success can still be found on wagon name plates discovered all over the world. Increased overseas competition was a major factor in the decline and closure of the firm which went into voluntary liquidation in 1928.

Iron works belonging to Wooton Brothers Ltd, *c.* 1960. The Wootton brothers came to the town from Loughborough in 1876 and set up a works to produce cast and forged items for the local mining and brick works and the company rapidly developed to gain a world wide reputation. At one time the works produced stationary steam engines under the name 'Charnwood'.

A Wootton's advertisement, *c.* 1920.

Mr Wootton and his workers, c. 1890. Many of these workers came from the Black Country and were sufficiently highly skilled to enable the development of a wide range of trade outlets. The company specialized in producing brick making and quarrying equipment.

Wootton's foundry, c. 1920. The works was capable of producing items up to 10 tons in weight which could then be finished in the adjacent, and well equipped, machine shop. Machines capable of producing 4,000 bricks per hour were made and sold all over the world.

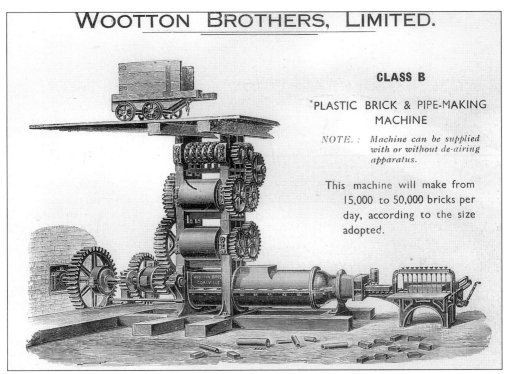

A Wootton's plastic brick and pipe machine advertisement, c. 1920. The works made a range of clay processing equipment, capable of making up to 60,000 bricks per day. They were able to undertake to fully equip a brick and pipe works anywhere in the world.

Firing a brick kiln, c. 1950. From 1840, new brick works were set up by a number of entrepreneurs, and by the local collieries, to take advantage of both the excellent clay deposits overlying the coal and availability of cheap, locally mined coal. Dozens of these circular down-draught kilns were in operation in the neighbourhood.

Workers at the Coalville Brick Co., *c.* 1940. A special bed of clay enabled this works, one of the later brickyards to open, to produce sand-stock bricks for use in the many aerodromes constructed in the Cotswolds and Lincolnshire areas in the inter-war years.

Advertisements such as this ensured that the very high quality bricks and terracotta produced in the town were used in the construction of many prestigious buildings in cities throughout the country.

'George Smith of Coalville', a prominent local Primitive Methodist, was employed as manager of the Whitwick Colliery tile works. Appalled by the conditions under which children and young women had to work in the brick and tile yards of England, he fought a single handed national campaign to highlight the problem which resulted in the passing of The Factory Act (Brick and Tile Yards) Extension Bill in 1871. Having led a further campaign which resulted in the passing of the Canal Boat Act in 1884, he turned his attention to the Gypsy population. Unfortunately he died without his proposed Movable Dwellings Bill passing into law.

Workers at Coalville mosaic tile and terracotta works, c. 1880. These workers produced a range of coloured tiles and terracotta which were much admired by Victorian house owners.

H.R. Mansfield with local Methodists, *c.* 1920. Mr Mansfield came to the town to set up the Hermitage Brick and Tile Co. He was a leading Methodist and is seen here at one of their conventions which were held at his elegant residence, Broomleys.

Mr Mansfield's election flyer in 1900. He was a prominent Liberal and was elected MP for Spalding in 1900 and again in 1906 but resigned in 1909 owing to pressure of business.

T. and J. Jones elastic web factory, *c*. 1928. Many females, put out of work by the passing of the Brickyard Act, found work here. Elastic-braided narrow fabrics were produced for the shoe and clothing industries. The factory was later taken over by Joseph Burgess and Sons Ltd.

Burgess's workers in the cord and braid shop, *c*. 1928.

Burgess's workers in the weaving shop, *c*. 1928.

The high proportion of young female labour can be seen in this Burgess workforce in 1928.

A Clutsom and Kemp loom shop, *c.* 1950. In 1909, the Highfields Weaving and Manufacturing Co. was set up by Mr Jones and Mr Kemp, two Coalville businessmen, and in 1916 they were joined by Charles Clutsom, an inventive man who was later to revolutionize narrow fabric manufacture with his development of the shuttleless loom. The company's name was changed to Clutsom and Kemp Ltd and they had become a major manufacturer of suspender elastic by 1918.

Mr Clutsom (far left), and his workers, *c.* 1914. By the 1950s the company had become a major manufacturer in the town, employing about 1,000 workers, and was the largest manufacturer of narrow fabrics in the world. Until the early 1960s the labour force was predominantly female. The company also produced large numbers of shuttleless looms for the manufacture of narrow fabric.

Bardon Quarry, *c*. 1880. Messrs Everard and Ellis expanded their stone quarrying business to nearby Bardon in 1857 and were soon producing large amounts of crushed granite for use in macadamizing roads. Stone sets and kerbings were also produced.

Bardon stone crushing mills, *c*. 1910. In 1873, the Granite Co. replaced its old mill with a new one, housing more powerful equipment and it was soon producing up to 4,000 tons of crushed stone a week.

Bardon steam lorries, *c.* 1920. Granite was mainly conveyed straight onto the Midland Railway by a private siding but for local customers stone was carried away by means of steam powered lorries.

Coalville munitions workers, *c.* 1916. Many females were put to work in munitions factories during the First World War. This one was sited in one of the many brick works in town.

Howard's cycle works, *c.* 1890. With improvements in road conditions, the bicycle became more widely used and in 1888 Messrs Howard & Co., engineers, turned their attention to the manufacture of their 'Newmarket' range of cycles.

Several thousands of these cycles were produced each year and were for sale at a price of £5 10s.

Coalville Working Men's Co-operative Society bakery, *c.* 1930. The first Co-op bakery was opened in 1898 to provide daily baked bread and confectioneries for its many customers in the district.

Coalville telephone exchange, *c.* 1914. The National Telephone Co. opened for business in 1907 operating nine lines from an exchange which was under the supervision of Miss Julia Stacey in the front room of a house in Park Road. Public calls could be made from a 'silence box' inside the front door.

Wolsey workers, *c.* 1928. Wolsey Ltd of Leicester opened an out-factory in Coalville which gave employment mainly to female workers from the district.

Coalville police force, *c.* 1920.

The first group of employees of Pegson's Co. Ltd. Samuel Pegg and Son of Leicester, part of the Mellor Bromley Group, came to Coalville in 1931 to take over the foundry of the former Stableford works and they formed the Pegson Co. Ltd. The workers seen here came from Leicester to help set up the firm which made quarry machinery.

The manufacture of Pegson stone crushers and naval guns, c. 1942. The company's production of stone crushers, seen on the right, was augmented during the war with armament production.

One of many hundreds of artillery guns made by Pegson's as their contribution to the war effort.

The largest primary gyratory stone crusher produced in the 1950s. After the war, the company became highly specialized in the production of quarry plant machinery. This is one of a number of stone crushers produced for major international projects such as the construction of the Owen Falls Dam in Uganda.

Spitfire 'Oleo' leg manufacture at the No. 10 factory, Cascelloid's, in Coalville, *c.* 1941. Owing to the disruption of manufacture caused by the Blitz of Birmingham, the production of Spitfire and Seafire parts was dispersed around the Midland counties. Coalville and the surrounding villages produced, among other components, virtually all the landing-wheel legs for these aircraft for the duration of the war.

The Palitoy exhibit at the British Industries Fair in 1952. In 1932, Cascelloid Ltd moved its production of plastic dolls from Leicester to a disused billiard hall in Coalville on a three and a half acre site. The factory was requisitioned during the war for production of anti-gas eye shields, Spitfire parts and bomb noses and tails made of laminated paper. After the war, the firm moved into plastic injection moulding for toys such as the famous 'Action Man'.

H. Blythe and Sons' garage, although by this time it had been taken over by Motors (Coalville) Ltd, *c.* 1937. As the mass market for cars began to develop in the 1920s, Blythe's became the main agent for Ford and provided extensive maintenance facilities. This lorry was supplied, through them, to Mr B. Bamkin in 1933 and six years later had covered 152,853 miles without needing a re-bore. It was reported to be running well and using negligible quantities of oil.

Another Blythe maintained lorry at the Ashby Show in 1935. Shown decorated as a trade float for entry in the show, the lorry was supplied for the carting of coal and continued in service for many years. A similar model was adapted as a breakdown truck. Note the competitive prices for coal in those difficult days of the 1930s.

Four

The Developing Town

Snibston Colliery, *c.* 1900. The view towards the town centre shows the end of Lower Snibston Buildings on the right and on the left are houses built for people involved in support trades such as blacksmiths, harness makers, tool sharpeners and rope makers. These houses also accommodated a beer house which, together with two public houses, provided refreshment for men coming off shift.

The 'Green Man', c. 1905. In 1896 a public urinal, made in cast iron and concrete, was erected in the town centre to provide comfort for the users of the market and the many public houses in town.

Looking east along High Street (formerly Station Street), c. 1910. The shops on the right were built as houses on land sold from the estate of William Stenson in 1861. The front rooms were gradually converted and developed into a very comprehensive range of shops. The buildings on the left were constructed earlier but some were improved in the 1890s.

Looking west along High Street, *c.* 1910. By this period the town had become a prosperous trade centre and in 1895 the Leicester Banking Company built their new bank, the imposing building shown on the left, to provide a better service for trades people. It later became the Midland Bank.

Looking west along Hotel Street, *c.* 1920. These houses, most with front rooms converted to shops, were built in the boom time of the 1860s. The building on the right was a printing works owned by the Holmes family.

Chapel Corner in 1906. The Baptist chapel and school were built at this junction of Long Lane and the road to Whitwick in 1836. An ancient farm stood here and Whitwick Colliery Co. sank a bore-hole for a village pump which, for many years, provided drinking water for this part of the developing town.

Looking east from the church along London Road, c. 1905. As the town prospered, housing was erected for middle class professionals and for trades people. The tree lined road contrasted sharply with other parts of the town.

Coalville Park, *c.* 1905. The land for the park was a gift from the Coalville Athletics Club to the inhabitants of the town; it was to be held in perpetuity from 8 March 1899 when it was handed over to the council. Athletics meetings previously held on the ground attracted large crowds and enabled the club to make the purchase in 1880.

Looking west along London Road, *c.* 1910. Coalville Cemetery, on the left, was opened in 1858. Side streets were developed in the last decade of the nineteenth century and the first decade of the twentieth century to house the families of workers arriving to gain employment in the developing engineering firms. Many of these families came from the West Midlands.

The Fox and Goose Inn, *c.* 1912. The inn stands at the east end of London Road and at one time defined the town's boundary. It was built with its attendant row of cottages in the 1830s. At the entrance to Charnwood Street stood a notice advertising the services of the Charnwood Forest Railway.

London Road, *c.* 1920. As the town continued to expand in the 1890s, houses were built in the open fields towards Bardon. On the left is an ancient farmhouse which stood in its own fields at this time.

Broom Leys House, c. 1900. The Whetstone family built this house, when they came from Leicester, in the chateau style as a very luxurious mansion in open countryside. It passed into the hands of the Mansfield family and during the First World War housed many men recovering from wounds received in France. Converted to a secondary vocational school of high repute in the 1920s, it is now a Leicestershire county primary school.

Forest Road was developed as the middle classes moved from the centre of Coalville at the end of the nineteenth century. W.D. Stableford and John Puxley-White, manager of the South Leicestershire Colliery Co., built considerable mansions, both of which later housed convents.

Varnham's Rows, looking south along Central Road towards Hugglescote, *c.* 1916. As workers' housing was needed, local entrepreneurs built terraces of houses along the roads leading to the former village parishes, thus increasing the physical size of the town. The houses seen here are typical examples built on Hugglescote Lane on either side of the Halfway Inn, halfway between Hugglescote and Whitwick. The parade was held in aid of a proposed Coalville hospital.

Coalville police station and law court, first on the left, *c.* 1920. This was situated on a part of Belvoir Road (originally Hugglescote Lane) called the White Leys and was built using the highest quality local bricks and terracotta. The ancient White Leys farm can be seen in the distance.

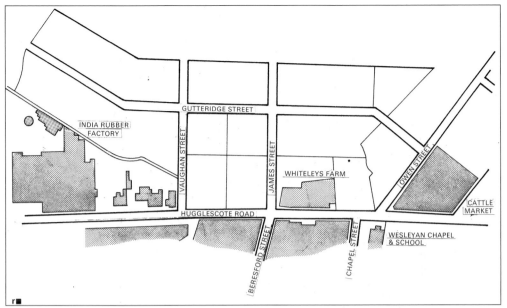

A plan of the proposed Gutteridge estate to be called the Highfields, *c.* 1900. The plan shows the extent of the estate built by James Gutteridge on White Leys' land in Snibston parish. James Gutteridge came to the town as a general dealer in the early days; however, he saw the potential of the area and reinvested his wealth in the town to develop the Highfields in the early part of this century.

St Faiths church, 'New Snibston', *c.* 1900. So many new families moved into the Highfields that the small parish church at Snibston could not cope and it was necessary to open this new church in 1900. It was constructed on a wooden framework to which woven wire was attached and into which gypsum plaster was cast.

St Saviour's Catholic church, *c.* 1900. This church was erected with a sense of urgency, out of wood and corrugated iron, in order to encourage development of Catholicism in the Highfields part of town. The building was very plain outside but had a highly decorated interior.

Belvoir Road and the Wesleyan Methodist chapel, halfway down the road on the right, *c.* 1915. Development of housing in side streets off Hugglescote Lane (known later as Belvoir Road) in the White Leys area of Coalville commenced in 1860 and gave reason for the construction of the Wesleyan chapel and adjacent day school in 1881.

The Primitive Methodist chapel and school of 1862 on Hugglescote Lane. The Primitive Methodists commenced worship in the Snibston Colliery school in 1832 but later moved, under the leadership of George Smith, to new and enlarged premises.

The Primitive Methodist chapel in the Newmarket, c. 1905. The congregation had outgrown its earlier church by the turn of the century and finally installed itself in the Newmarket in a church capable of holding 600 worshippers.

Marlborough Square, *c.* 1900. By this time the cattle market in the Newmarket area had been moved to make way for more prestigious buildings including the public hall, the Primitive Methodist chapel and the Coalville Working Men's Co-operative Society store. A large town square was also constructed and named Marlborough Square.

Coalville Public Hall, *c.* 1908. This hall was built to hold 500 people in 1876 at a cost of £1,800. It was used for civic occasions and for a wide variety of entertainment. It was renamed the Theatre Royal and was eventually converted into a cinema called the Electric Theatre, in 1910.

Looking north along Hugglescote Lane towards the Green Man, *c.* 1895. The houses on the right were constructed in 1861 and were gradually converted into shops. The shops on the left were built in about 1880 to provide the higher quality produce now required by the more varied population.

The Memorial Clock Tower from Belvoir Road, *c.* 1930. The central crossroads had been considerably improved by the removal of the 'Green Man' and the construction of the Memorial Clock Tower in 1925.

A view east from the Memorial Clock Tower along High Street and Hotel Street, *c*. 1930. This picture shows the extent of development over the first 100 years. The tall building on the right was the Leicestershire Bank which later became the Midland Bank.

A view south from the Memorial Clock Tower along Belvoir Road, *c*. 1978. The Snibstone New Inn (right) and the Royal Oak Inn (left) are in the foreground.

Five
Special Events

An open air meeting in the Newmarket to celebrate Queen Victoria's Golden Jubilee. The Primitive Methodist church, built in 1865, can be seen in the background. The houses on the right were known as Bug and Flea Row.

The Fox and Goose Hotel, *c*. 1887. This garland archway was constructed to celebrate Queen Victoria's Golden Jubilee.

A parade of the local dignitaries at the Baptist chapel celebrating the Golden Jubilee.

Station Street, decorated for the Golden Jubilee. The houses on the left, built in 1861, were progressively converted into shops. The houses on the right were of earlier vintage with the Bell Inn (known later as the Blue Bell) on the extreme right.

A parade marking Queen Victoria's Diamond Jubilee passes the Engineers Arms and public hall in 1897.

A disaster occurred at the Whitwick Colliery on 19 April 1898. Thirty-five men died underground, killed by toxic gases from an underground fire raging in No. 5 pit. The townspeople were awakened by the sound of the colliery hooter in the early hours of the morning and are seen here waiting anxiously as a body is brought to the surface by the rescuers.

As time went by, large crowds of people continued to gather to express sympathy for families who had lost their men, or to await news of those still trapped.

From time to time, bodies were brought to the surface and taken in hearses, by local funeral directors, to the mortuary as crowds continued to gather.

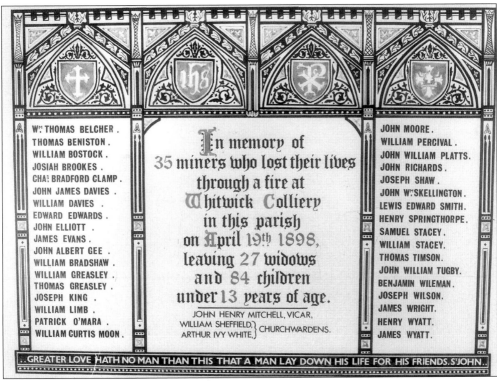

Wᵐ THOMAS BELCHER .
THOMAS BENISTON .
WILLIAM BOSTOCK .
JOSIAH BROOKES .
CHAˢ BRADFORD CLAMP .
JOHN JAMES DAVIES .
WILLIAM DAVIES .
EDWARD EDWARDS .
JOHN ELLIOTT .
JAMES EVANS .
JOHN ALBERT GEE .
WILLIAM BRADSHAW .
WILLIAM GREASLEY .
THOMAS GREASLEY .
JOSEPH KING .
WILLIAM LIMB .
PATRICK O'MARA .
WILLIAM CURTIS MOON .

In memory of
35 miners who lost their lives
through a fire at
Whitwick Colliery
in this parish
on April 19th 1898,
leaving 27 widows
and 84 children
under 13 years of age.
JOHN HENRY MITCHELL, VICAR,
WILLIAM SHEFFIELD,⎱ CHURCHWARDENS.
ARTHUR IVY WHITE,⎰

JOHN MOORE .
WILLIAM PERCIVAL .
JOHN WILLIAM PLATTS .
JOHN RICHARDS .
JOSEPH SHAW .
JOHN Wᵐ SKELLINGTON .
LEWIS EDWARD SMITH .
HENRY SPRINGTHORPE .
SAMUEL STACEY .
WILLIAM STACEY .
THOMAS TIMSON .
JOHN WILLIAM TUGBY .
BENJAMIN WILEMAN .
JOSEPH WILSON .
JAMES WRIGHT .
HENRY WYATT .
JAMES WYATT .

.. GREATER LOVE HATH NO MAN THAN THIS THAT A MAN LAY DOWN HIS LIFE FOR HIS FRIENDS. Sᵗ JOHN ..

A memorial tablet to those who perished in the colliery disaster.

A meet of the Quorn Hunt at the Fox and Goose Hotel in 1895. The countryside was still a part of the town until the turn of the new century.

The official opening of Coalville Park in May 1900. In the 1880s, a flourishing athletics club purchased land to the north of London Road and organized athletics events over the next twenty years to raise the price of £3,000. In 1899, they gave part of the land to the town for the construction of a pleasure park, providing that no ball games would be played on it.

A Band of Hope march from Coalville Park in 1909. A thousand members of temperance groups from the local churches assembled in the park before marching around the many public houses in the town to highlight the evils of drink.

Band of Hope protesters outside the Gate Inn at Hugglescote.

The organizing committee of Hugglescote Annual Flower Show, *c.* 1910. This was always a major attraction for the area and produced intense competition.

A Sunday schools rally, *c.* 1911. Every year, the many Sunday schools in town paraded around the town to a meeting in Marlborough Square.

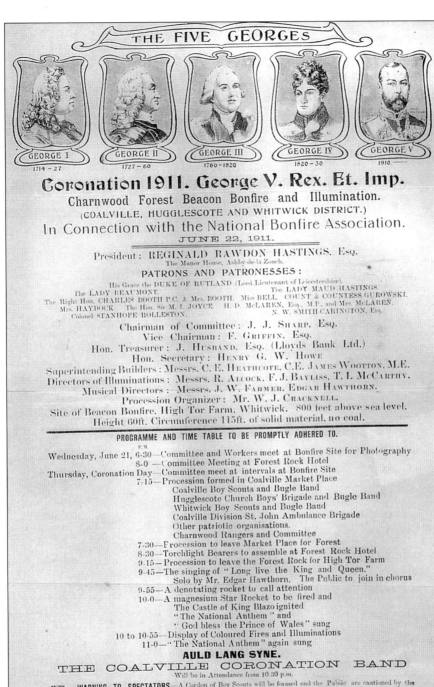

The coronation of King George V was celebrated in style by the townsfolk, culminating in a torch-lit procession to the ceremonial lighting of a large bonfire. A poster gave details of the arrangements.

The bonfire was built by the local Royal Ancient Order of Buffaloes and the Charnwood Forest Rangers.

The first set of pupils to attend Coalville Grammar School in 1909. Before this school was built, pupils had to travel to Ashby-de-la-Zouch or Loughborough to gain a grammar school education.

Coalville Working Men's Co-operative Society's children's treat in 1912. This annual treat was, on this occasion, attended by 6,000 children who marched behind bands from several of the Co-op branch stores to a grand sports day and tea party. They consumed 12,000 bars of chocolate, 14,000 food packs, 2,000 lbs of cake and 920 gallons of tea. The band can be seen leading the parade from the Marlborough Square store.

Burgess's factory fire, 6 April 1917. This day proved to be a disastrous day for the town. A fire at Burgess's factory put many local women's jobs at risk and, in the same weekend, many people in town were made ill when the local Co-op bakery mixed mineral oil instead of vegetable oil into their hot cross buns.

A recruiting parade for the First World War marching in Central Road.

The first batch of recruits leaving Coalville station at the beginning of the First World War.

Horses were commandeered from Coalville Co-operative Society and are seen here being loaded at Coalville station goods depot for dispatch to the Western Front in 1914.

In 1916, wounded British and Belgian soldiers were tended in the comfort of Broomleys House by army nurses and local volunteers.

The first memorial to the dead of the First World War, *c.* 1919. A plaque listing the 'Fallen of the Great War' was unveiled in High Street and was built into the boundary wall of the railway station.

The Memorial Clock Tower, *c.* 1946. The memorial was unveiled by Mrs Charles Booth, in the presence of 10,000 people. The clock tower was built in brick and stood sixty-eight feet tall; it was erected in the centre of the town in memory of the dead of the two world wars and the names are recorded in lead lettering affixed to tablets of Cornish granite.

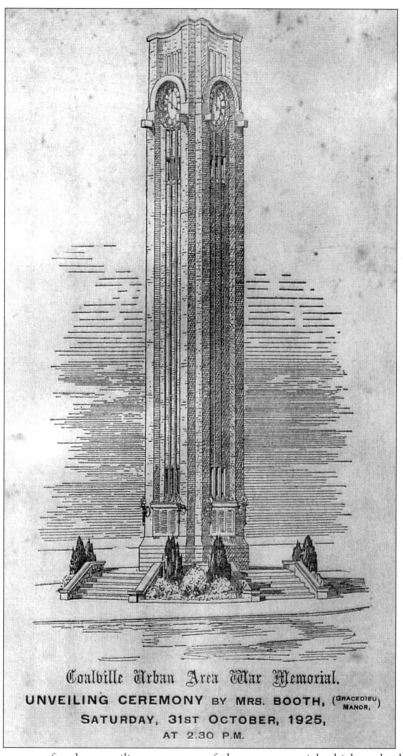

Coalville Urban Area War Memorial.
UNVEILING CEREMONY BY MRS. BOOTH, (GRACEDIEU MANOR,)
SATURDAY, 31ST OCTOBER, 1925,
AT 2.30 P.M.

The programme for the unveiling ceremony of the war memorial which took place on 31 October 1925.

The support committee for striking miners at the adult school in 1921. A committee was set up in town to provide help, in the form of soup kitchens, for families suffering the effects of the miners lockout.

Local miners' agent, Jack Smith, travelled south in a gypsy caravan pulled by a horse to put the miners' case to a wider public and to raise funds for the miners' families.

The Coalville Lion handbook for the Hospital Carnival in 1939. The lion story dominated talk in town for several weeks. A local resident was retiring for the night and had cause to look out of his bedroom window. He observed in his garden a large animal which moved stealthily through the entry into the street and went through other gardens before disappearing. The following morning he reported his sighting of a lion and people were too scared to go out until the lion was identified as having been a donkey.

The Carnival Queen and attendants in 1939.

THE CARNIVAL DAY BY DAY

ALL EVENTS ON CARNIVAL FIELD, BELVOIR ROAD (Except where otherwise stated)

APPROXIMATE TIME-TABLE

FRIDAY

		see page
6-0	"Rag" Assembles	36
6-45	Procession to Field	21
7-0	Crowning of Queen	21
7-30	Folk Dancing	21
8-0	Variety Show (Progressive Hall)	19
8-0	Ladies' Football Match	21
8-0	The Queen and her Attendants visit Ellistown	13
8-30	Comedy Turn by section of "Rag"	36
9-0	Comic Bands Display	
9-30	Dancing and Community Singing	17

Throughout the day collectors will be in the streets and the fun-making "Rough Riders" will also be about.

SATURDAY

		see page
11-30	Queen and Attendants tour Whitwick	13
2-30	Parade and Carnival Bands assemble in Memorial Sq.	13
3-0	Parade moves off	13
4-30	Carnival Band Contest	38
7-30	Variety Show on Field	19
8-30	Presentation of Prizes	
8-40	Winning Band and Queen and Attendants parade town	13
9-0	Dancing and Community Singing	17

SUNDAY

2-30	Church Parade and Drum Head Service. Local Public Bodies will attend.
8-0	Concert in Marquee on the Carnival Field.

MONDAY

		see pa
10-30	Queen and Attendants tour Hugglescote and Ravenstone	
11-0	Boxing (Town F.C. Ground)	
2-30	Parade and Brass Bands assemble Memorial Square	
3-0	Parade moves off	
4-0	Brass Band Contest	
4-0—4-30	Rex Reader, the famous illusionist, will drive a car blindfold on the Carnival Field	
6-0	"Queen of Charnwood" Competition	
7-0	Tug-of-War	
7-30	Variety Show on Field	
8-0	Presentation of Prizes	
9-0	Dancing and Community Singing	

TUESDAY

		see p
2-0	Queen and Attendants visit Bardon	
2-30	Baby Show	
3-0	Punch and Judy Show	
3-30	Children's Sports	
5-0	Dog and Pet Show	
5-30	Keep-Fit Display	
6-0	Punch and Judy Show	
7-30	Amateur Boxing	
8-0	Variety Show (Progressive Hall)	
8-30	Presentation of Prizes	
9-0	Dancing and Community Singing	
10-0	Torchlight Procession	

ATTRACTIONS AND COMPETITIONS EVERY DAY
CONCLUDING WITH OPEN-AIR DANCING AND COMMUNITY SINGING

Additional Amusements will be made known

ADMISSION EVERY DAY 3d.   Children 1d.

The programme of events for the 1939 carnival.

Coalville hospital parade in 1930. The accidents that occurred in the many heavy industries of the town indicated the real need for a local hospital and carnival events were organized annually to raise funds. The parade is shown here in Forest Road, with Snibston Colliery's prize winning band providing martial music for the parade.

The parade passed through the main housing areas of the town, such as Highfields. After the First World War, interest grew and a week long carnival was held in May every year to raise funds to build a hospital but this goal was not achieved until 1988 when these funds were reclaimed and contributed to the new NHS hospital.

The carnival parade dispersed on reaching its destination in Marlborough Square.

The opening of the new YMCA huts in Memorial Square, c. 1928. Interest in the YMCA was generated by the local churches in the early part of the twentieth century and meetings were initially held in one of the local chapels. Its first independent meeting room was leased above the post office in Hotel Street, in 1909, but as membership grew new, larger premises were needed.

The opening of the Coalville public baths on 23 June 1929. The Leicestershire District Miners' Welfare Committee built the baths at a cost of £18,097 on land provided by the council, and handed them over to the council in perpetuity. The miners donated one penny from their payment for each ton of coal turned locally. The baths were built by W. Moss and Son and several members of that family appear in the photograph.

The opening of the new offices of Coalville Urban District Council in 1934. The two Miss Higgins presented flowers to Mrs Blower, wife of the chairman of the county council, and to Mrs Brown, wife of the chairman of the town council. Initially the council had offices above the Leicestershire Bank but it was found necessary to build the new municipal offices on London Road at a cost of £14,000.

Coalville Urban District Council's first sitting in the new offices on 3 January 1935. The council was formed in 1894 from the surrounding parishes and included members representing the developing town.

Celebrations in Broughton Street at the end of the War in Europe.

Members of a street party from Park Road celebrate the end of the War with Japan in 1945.

The Youth Sunday march in 1945.

The Victory issue of *The Billet*, published in 1945. *The Billet* was produced throughout the war to keep serving men in touch with home news and with each other. The publication was produced by local newsman Jack Hussey and Mrs Dorothy Harris, the 'unknown lady', and they sent copies regularly to all fields of operation. Mrs Harris addressed 250,000 envelopes during the war to send 2,000 of the 8,000 copies produced each month to serving people. The other 6,000 were sold locally by relatives

Six

Entertainment

Coalville munitions ladies football team, winners of the Bass Charity Vase, in 1918. Owing to the absence of so many men who were fighting in the war, the local football leagues and competitions were abandoned. Therefore, women's teams were set up. A team of young ladies employed in the local munitions factory joined and comprehensively won a Midlands knock-out competition and in so doing raised funds for a local hospital.

Ebenezer chapel Brass Band, *c.* 1899. Many miners played in several brass bands, one of which practised in the chapel near to Snibston Colliery. The band had many members from one family, the Benistones. Another local band was named the '7 Bs' since they were the 'Best Blooming Brass Band Between Burton and Bagworth' – Bagworth was a nearby pit village.

A performance of *The Messiah* at the Ebenezer Baptist chapel *c.* 1905. The chapel was famous for the quality of its music and had its own orchestra and a choir which numbered over one hundred.

Snibston Colliery Brass Band, *c.* 1936. Developed from the Ebenezer Band, this colliery band eventually gained a national reputation and won many prizes.

Coalville Philharmonic Orchestra, *c.* 1935. This orchestra, comprising of local musicians under the leadership of Frank Newman, gave regular performances in the Baths Hall which was formed when the swimming baths were boarded over in the winter months.

Coalville Amateur Operatic Society's performance of *The Gondoliers, c.* 1930. Music played a very important part in entertaining the townsfolk. The society's annual performance continues to be eagerly anticipated and performances are usually sold out.

Coalville Junior Choir, *c.* 1920. Choral singing started at a young age, many of the children being trained in the art for the Chapel Sermons (anniversary days). Both this choir and a flourishing children's choir, sponsored by the Coalville Co-op, won many trophies.

The Sheringham Singers, *c*. 1948. Many children in Coalville trained in the junior choirs and eventually graduated to one of the male voice choirs, church choirs or senior choirs such as the Sheringham Singers.

The Coalville Electric Theatre, *c*. 1905. The public hall had been used for many civic occasions and also for the presentation of plays produced by travelling repertory companies. In 1910, the building was converted into the Coalville Electric Theatre by Mr Johnson. In order to ensure a regular attendance, many films featuring silent movie stars were shown in twenty-six episodes and were accompanied by a pianist. The Electric Theatre was taken over and much improved by Mr Deeming in 1920 who renamed it The Grand.

The Grand's staff outing, *c.* 1935. These employees were about to leave from The Grand on the annual staff outing arranged by Mr Deeming.

Coalville Olympia, *c.* 1920. A skating rink was opened here by Coalville Olympia Company in February 1910 but this was later converted, first into a repertory theatre and then equipped as Mr Deeming's second cinema.

The demolition of Olympia, *c*. 1933. In order to provide up to date facilities Mr Deeming built the Regal cinema on the site of Olympia. It was later used as a Casino club.

The Rex Cinema, *c*. 1938. Such were the demands of film goers that the Rex cinema, built to the highest standards of the day, was also opened in Marlborough Square in 1938.

The Vagabonds' concert party, *c.* 1930. Many small groups of young people set up their own entertainment parties to amuse people in their churches and clubs.

Coalville Baptist cricket team, *c.* 1890. Participating in sport was a popular activity in the town and there were many cricket and football teams, a flourishing athletics club and a cycle club. The cricketer (third from the right, back row) was W.D. Stableford.

Coalville Cottagers' horticultural committee at the opening of the Annual Flower and Vegetable Show, *c.* 1910. The committee raised hundreds of pounds for Leicester Royal Infirmary and for a convalescent home built in nearby Charnwood Forest.

Coalville Swifts football club, *c.* 1926.

Coalville cycle club, *c.* 1912.

The town has produced a number of
international footballers, the most famous
of which was Hughie Adcock who played
for Leicester City and England.

Seven

Education

Wesleyan school infants demonstrating their knitting skills, *c.* 1900.

A reunion of the Baptist 'British Scholars' in 1915. Coalville Baptist school was enlarged in 1858 and run on the model of a British School. It provided an excellent education for working class children initially at a fee of 1d per week. A list of ex-scholars prepared for the reunion demonstrated the achievements of individuals, then living in many parts of the world. They included ten business proprietors, nine headmasters, five editors, two bank managers, two principals, two solicitors, a chartered accountant and a doctor.

The Wesleyan senior boys class of 1925, with the headmaster, Mr Thomas Frith, on the left. The Wesleyan Methodists opened a school on Belvoir Road in 1875. The building was also used for worship until the chapel was built alongside in 1881. The school was enlarged and an infants' department was added in 1896. The school thus accommodated 420 pupils and 345 infants.

All Saints' Church of England school, Standard 1 class, *c.* 1895. Children of Anglican families attended the Church National School opened in 1838, but with the closure of the British School in 1894, it was necessary to open a further school in the west end of town. All Saints school opened in 1895 with eighty-nine pupils.

The Nicholls and Billings families, *c.* 1898. The children of these families lived at The Bricklayers Arms, a beer house opposite Snibston Colliery, and were among the first to attend the new All Saints' school.

Children of the Baptist school at Hugglescote, *c.* 1900. Many children from the houses being developed in the south of the town attended here.

Bridge Road county school. By 1904, all the local schools were full to overflowing and it was necessary to build another school. Bridge Road school, which included a secondary department, was built in Bridge Road to accommodate 550 pupils in 1908.

Bridge Road school staff, including headmaster Mr Harris, at the first Christmas party.

Bridge Road school gardening class, *c.* 1915. Older pupils were taught practical skills such as gardening, carpentry and cookery.

Coalville Grammar School. Pupils no longer had to travel to other towns for a grammar school education after the town opened its own grammar school in 1909.

An early group of grammar school pupils with headmaster Mr Storr-Best, *c.* 1913.

An arson attempt nearly destroyed the grammar school in 1984.

THE SACRED HEART CONVENT OF THE SISTERS OF ST DOROTHY, COALVILLE.

St Dorothy's Convent school, *c.* 1920. A school was opened by the Sisters of St Dorothy on Forest Road in the former residence of the manager of the South Leicester Colliery Company.

A gymnastic display at Bridge Road junior school on Empire Day in 1935. Pupils from the newly built county primary and junior school displayed their skills.

Coalville Grammar School's performance of *Caesar's Friend*, c. 1946.

Eight

Trade and Commerce

Mr Stacey photographing High Street, *c.* 1947. He was the town's photographer for many years and was renowned for the quality of his studio portraits.

CATTLE MARKET,

COALVILLE.

57 BEASTS

5 FAT & STORE CALVES

181 SHEEP & LAMBS,

166 Bacon, Porket, & Store PIGS,

Horses, Poultry, Cheese, &c.

TO BE SOLD BY AUCTION, BY

ORCHARD & SON

TUESDAY, SEPT. 19th, 1893.

Sale will commence at 11-0 prompt.

☞ The Auctioneers urgently request Vendors to assist them in Starting the Sale Punctually, by having Stock on the Ground in good time.

Jas. Goadby & Son, Printers, Ashby-de-la-Zouch.

An advertisement for the cattle market, in 1893. The first cattle market was held at the rear of the Red House, conveniently situated near the railway station. Trade grew rapidly though, and the site of the market was removed to the White Leys area and renamed the Newmarket. Later, as that area was developed commercially, the market returned to an enlarged site at the Olde Red House.

Coalville Market, *c.* 1920. The market grew rapidly around the central crossroads and spread into the surrounding streets. It attracted people from as far away as Leicester in the east and the villages of South Derbyshire in the west, indeed anyone who could travel by train, horse and later by bus. The market was open on Fridays from 7.30 am to 9.30 pm and was illuminated by oil flares in the darkness of the winter months.

Looking east along High Street, *c.* 1900. The early inhabitants of the town obtained their supplies from traders in the four villages but as the population grew general dealers began to arrive to serve the people from shops built along Station Street near to the Olde Red House. The houses built on the south side of Station Street, in 1861, were soon converted into of shops of all kinds.

Amos' Saddlery, Harness and Athletics Depot, c. 1905. This shop was opened in the front rooms of a house on Station Street (known later as High Street) around 1876 and developed to serve the needs of the many horse owners in the town and district.

Looking west along High Street, c. 1925. A great variety of shops had, by now, occupied the fronts of the houses along the length of High Street. Attempts to introduce three storey premises were stalled by the First World War and the subsequent depression in local trade.

The shops in Hotel Street, *c.* 1920. Houses that had been built on the south side of Hotel Street in the 1860s had been converted to shops by the 1890s. The garage was one of several opened in the early 1900s to serve the car owner, the new mode of transport which had already begun to replace the horse.

Coalville Working Men's Co-operative Society opened a shop in the front room of a terraced house in 1882 despite much opposition from other traders. In ten years it had a membership of 800 and a share capital of £3,200. A move into the Newmarket area proved successful and, with a turnover of £306,000, they built their fourth town centre premises in 1916.

The opening of Coalville Working Men's Co-operative Society's Hugglescote branch in 1902. The Co-op's success was so marked that many branch shops were built in newly developing areas of the expanding town and in the surrounding villages.

The Co-op delivery van, *c.* 1920. Goods were delivered to the customer's door throughout the district.

COLEMAN & SONS. IRONMONGERS & IMPLEMENT AGENTS. COALVILLE

Coleman & Sons' agricultural display, *c.* 1920. The family opened their hardware and furniture shop in the Newmarket in 1899. They also became distributors for, 'refined American petroleum', in 1904.

Roughton's chemist and druggist in 1916. One of the shops on Belvoir Road was occupied by Mr and Mrs Roughton, both of whom were qualified chemists. They dispensed the usual range of medicines and proprietary drugs but also, as Quakers, provided herbal medicines free of charge to the poor of the town.

Looking south along Belvoir Road towards Coleman's Corner and Marlborough Square *c.* 1925.

Looking south along Belvoir Road, *c.* 1940. All the houses on the east side of Belvoir Road had now had their front rooms converted into shops providing an immense choice of merchandise for the population.

A train about to leave Coalville railway station, c. 1960. By the turn of the twentieth century, Coalville had two railway stations and it was possible to travel north, south-east and west by train. Besides the normal traffic, many special trains were run to the seaside at holiday times.

A 'Sentinel' steam car at Whitwick railway station, c. 1910. In 1906, a Motor Rail service connected Coalville with Loughborough, via the Charnwood Forest Railway and with Shackerstone, via the Midland and LNW Joint Railway.

The Birmingham Midland Red Company opened its garage on Ashby Road in 1925.

Midland Red garage staff, *c.* 1930.

124

Charles Mann's 'Pride of the Forest' at Whitwick, *c.* 1920. This was one of the earliest buses owned by the company operating from its base in Whitwick. Midland Red bought the firm in 1934.

C.W. Shaw's 'Greyhound' coach at the Memorial Clock Tower, *c.* 1930. This twenty-six-seater 'Reo' bus operated from 1928 to 1931. In 1937, this became another company which was bought out by Midland Red.

A Brown's Blue Daimler double-decker in Marlborough Square. The company ran many services in the district and acquired several other operators.

Blockley's 'Ruby' Dennis coach at Hettons Row, Ashby Road, c. 1960. The company ran a service to the nearby villages of Heather and Ibstock. The bus, JU 1000, was registered before the Second World War.

Victory Coaches' sole double-decker bus. Based at Ibstock, the company's buses were regularly used to transfer miners from surrounding villages to the collieries. This vehicle is an AEC Regent.

Oliver Bishop's Bedford coach in 1957. The company, which began in 1925, operated for many years from its garage in Owen Street until it was sold to another local firm, Bancroft and Powers, in 1973.

Whetton's 'The Ellen' bus standing in Memorial Square, *c.* 1930.

Cobham's Air display at Coalville in the mid 1930s. Blythe and Sons sponsored a children's essay writing competition and the first prize was a flight in one of the planes. Whether the winner took up the prize in view of the date of the event is not known.